by Eileen Myles

The Irony of the Leash (1978)
A Fresh Young Voice from the Plains (1981)
Sappho's Boat (1982)
Bread & Water (1987)
1969 (1989)
Not Me (1991)
Chelsea Girls (1994)
Maxfield Parrish/Early & New Poems (1995)
School of Fish (1997)

beneficial, deficient, superficial, wolfish efficiency, elfish, sufficient, fission, stand-offish, microfiche, fissure, officious, oafish, proficient, official, sacrificial, selfish, waifish

SCHOOL
OF
FISH

EILEEN
MYLES

BLACK SPARROW PRESS   SANTA ROSA   1997

ACKNOWLEDGMENTS

Some of these poems originally appeared in *American Poetry Review*, *Apex of M*, *Caught in the Act*, *Chelsea*, *Gas*, *A Gathering of the Tribes*, *Jejeune*, *Jiffy Boog*, *Koja*, *Long Shot*, *Meschabe*, *Nedge*, *Poets Say Goodbye to the 20th Century*, *Prosodia*, *Revolutionary Grrrl*, *Shiny*, *13th Moon*, *Torque*, *The Williamsburg Worm*, *The Zenith of Desire*. To all these inspired editors and the photographer Dona McAdams this poet says Thank You.

"Kurt" was written on a pair of torn jeans which were auctioned off to benefit PS 122 in New York, June 1996.

Cover art by Kay Rosen.

Thanks to Terry Lopez for the special typesetting on the cover.

Black Sparrow Press books are printed on acid-free paper.

LIBRARY OF CONGRESS CATALOGING-IN-PUBLICATION DATA

Myles, Eileen, 1949-
  School of Fish / Eileen Myles
      p.   cm.
  ISBN 1-57423-031-X (pbk. : alk. paper) — ISBN 1-57423-032-8 (cloth trade : alk. paper) — ISBN 1-57423-033-6 (signed cloth : alk. paper)
      1. City and town life—Poetry.   2. Lesbians—Poetry.   3. Women
      —Poetry.   I. Title
  PS3563.Y498S38   1997
  811'.54—dc21   97-11773
                                                                      CIP

for David Rattray

Table of Contents

1

SCHOOL OF FISH

1

The Troubador

I sing this
silly little solo
in the thundering
blue, in the
towers of
the church

suppose
you know
I've taken
poison. Know
the Spring we
had last
year. That
was my
last

These lights are
nice

let me warble
like a nice
sad bird
if a bird

had knees
& sense
to kneel
in the
light. Winter
wounds
me. Nothing
inside
to make
resistance.
I soar
I soar inside.

I saw that
lighter. I never
miss a living
trick. It's
my last
winter. Never
again see
so much
white. I've
hit the
ceiling now
& the branches
of your
heart. This
death is

yours. Feel
it, taste
it. My
female victory
in the
face of
power. Diva
means I
like the
cold. Though
I collapse
I blaze
inside. The
deathlike
chimes
remind
my heart
the lull
the peaks
are mine.
Now he is singing
so far off.
My male side. I
fall in the towers
dark gleam. His
hordes of
men with
voices like

hair. No
women go
before. The tut tut
of the horns
say it's so
as I trill
between their
towers. I'm
standing
in a mouth
massive
as the tooth audience
grins. His voice
is like my
vanishing
soul. Hear the
melancholy
roll of
that hill
he's Spring
now, it's
heart, voice
I flutter
in my red blue
everything's
tower, this
mud of
mine moment

it's invisible
I entwine
my death.
Turning I come
she's gone.

Name the
feelings, stroll
around

she leaps to near me
dear so
unaccountably
& all
our paces quicken,
tumbling

peppered
by her
touch on
my leg
cooking
she comes
around
down on
the ground
she's so
beautiful

she's like
death. I'm
pumping
my men squinting in
pallor, polishing
black

horns
she opens
such delicacy
my thoughts
motives
hold her
sway.

A conversation
must take
place. Be
mine. Oh
oozing so

Turning she
sees me on the stair
lesbian
her hands
cut the air
we point two
ways. Perfect

design. He
doesn't
know I die.
It's almost
frisky our
gap. I remember
other seasons
Summer
oh that
Spring

I've got him to a fine
melt now.

June won't
do. Hope
you know
he's dying now
we gesture out.

The towers
more like candles
really. Pumpkins

a warmth
collides. A stray
figure, red
in front of the

heater. Where's
our death

he steps, he turns, he grabs

his crotch
she wails
his heart

The hands thunder
slapping, waving.

We need not live
in every dimension
he prays, he
sings   Did I

ever live here.
                    They grab
each other

Spring skips,
knows

this is beauty
a flowing rag
so much
blood, woman

stain down
my garment
I'm dying
love, feeling
belly burst
I'm another
old piece
of dirt
facing her
drain.

I know Sunday
she sings. I had
a home.
She thinks of his sad
little box. Scarred
by pebbles. Who
do you think you
are, I die

he sings. Nature
is beautiful now.
Think of my knees
she weeps. My
curving ankles
think how you stabbed
me last night

think how I
bled. It's
growing dark
Love

his arms wrap
her shoulders
the little angel
ready to fly
off. Everybody
knows. Oh I wish I
were her.

He is a man like history
Look out, another
day. See the birds

he see women
birds, women
suddenly she
dies

this is impossible
the warriors exclaim
more lovers
another madonna

Pretty, she took his

hand. Big
band. It's all
lips and snout
she is breast
& reach. Dad!
His heart breaks
& she she's my angel

two dying birds together
the cage is art
she soars
Man head in hands

she's suggesting
it's approximate

is there any such thing as a man?
Only a baby
They only die.
Now everyone
lying down, standing
up. Death is beautiful.

there is nothing
we sing
pull yourselves together
I have a brain tumor
I have taken poison

what about her?
she was burned at the stake
she screams
perhaps she utters
like tiny delicate
steps

who sees us?
it's culture
now. God is snoring.
Here he goes
baritone.
Pom pah
Pom pah
god is gentle
life is not

I'm only 40
liar
there's five of us now
How did we
start. 5
We're five again.
Not a 3
not a four
oh everyone
we're five now
two are lit.

two come to

reach & lift
they hold the
man. Woman
falling slow,
gone now lights
towers withdrawn
don't leave
me. Dawn
& you are meant
to die. The
fire is
lit
& so is
the sky.

43

Look at this my face in shock
body rapt, face of a clown
the room I'm nestled in
& your disarming sweetness
& the dog's breath
the lamp's too bright, certainly
costs more the plumbing draws its
breath yet again
the trucks unfurling flags
I want to know how you
inhabit your room or
as you're walking under the sun
a population sound or drowned in
habit. I miss him, last year.

Effigy

At home
when a small
brown
head
appeared
on the
handle
of a
whacker
that I lean
on the bookcase
I simply
leaned
closer
it's just
some kind
of old metal
clamp,
not a
face yet
the space
I'm leaning
in is
floundering

around
tugging
closer
to that
skull
empty eyes
that lolling
stuck-out
tongue.

Road Warrior

What happens when you
contain the flame?

I stuck my head out
the window &
waved at the stars.

Wait for me, I'm coming.
I'm coming home.

School of Fish

Everything's equal now. Blue leash blue bike
blue socks covering my ankles today
what about my friend: "I never wear socks"
for a week or two she lived in the streets &
it was such an illumination. What's this human
addiction to light. One morning I dreamt about
homelessness, joked about it. Life reduced
or expanded to getting doggie her very
next can. Dog's inexcusable addiction to
eating. At the bottom of the sea, David said,
the fishies are inexcusably addicted to light.
Same day I and my dog were left on the street.
No home, no keys, streams of pouring grey
rain. Now what is this grey, in relationship
to blue. Ask some painter is it less light
or is it what. What kind of hat should
I have worn yesterday in my crisis.
The dog's blue leash was gone. My feet reaching
over the bounds of the sidewalks, its curbs
and waves, pavement splashing up
hard and grey. Where did I see that man?

Someplace so human they even had one of *them*.
In a dark blue teeshirt, laughing. There is nothing
to my anecdote, my predicament, my color
crisis. There is nothing but blue & grey.
A glint hits the golden key, and it's a bad one
not the original and I kept turning and turning
there were copies everywhere in the neighborhood
that's what I am trying to say. I simply walked
and the apologies kept coming streaming in
and I said I simply walked and the tree
turned, no the key and the bottom of the sea
is flooded with light, we just get used to it
the deeper and deeper we go and the harder
it is to turn the key and eventually we
go and it is very very dark
we just get used to the light
but the blues and the greys and the feelings
of lostness, it's like home, it's like family.

The Open & the Close

It's the openness of summer
that perturbs me. Yeah, here comes
fall. Arranging the dark outlines
of my brown things in
a pitcher that looks
like it's at least used to green
but it's old itself, everything's
old, but not old enough.
In the morning I feel one
shrill breeze, it parts
the rest, even the brilliance
of mid afternoon,
its lamby laughing green
eye seems fated. The dog
curls, easier than
leaps. The honking geese
can have their useless
heyday, soon they'll just
be patterns on a sheet
though who could forget
their green shit. All
the bright flowers are
growing away & earlier
in the purple damp

moment of Iris
hopeful I climbed
back to the car that
curled through
greyness to stone &
its mountainous grief
the City, whose
icy winds, so silver
and smart, look
great & halfway
up it's clouds

and a breeze
hits my knee &
my lips & the
dog sees & it's
present, yellow

but the brown
threads down
the orange holds
it's dinnertime
little apples are spilled
on the stone
my pages flutter

Notice

The feathery horns of 21
geese and 10 ducks say
my dog is the scariest
thing on four legs
chewing away on her rawhide
frisbee millions and millions
of lily pads free
stretching the ample loop
of Towhee the genuine
name of a man-made
lake the fake
looks awfully natural
the algae working on
Rosie's fur
her hair falling out
the dark patch the geese
congregate in a reflection
of trees beyond the blue
begins again a stream
of darkening—trees
from the other side
into which
some boats are poking
around the naked

pink back of one of
the men his friend with
his teeshirt on
the voice of his
son in a bright yellow
jacket, save him
the ducks & the geese
are milling around
their black necks
ducking into the reflection
they're splashing breaking it up
into blue circles
again, real, it settles
then black again
with natural influences,
trees. My dog
struts out to
stalk them
she's surrounded by circles
she drinks
she looks
the white geese have
the deepest sound
I wonder why
leaders it seems
the dog walking over
she never catches them
on their own turf

mainly circles
getting her paws wet
bending down
dog on target
focus
turning around
clumps of family
feeding the geese
Rosie runs
the children scream
all the people turning around
honk honk a peaceful
quiet cooing everyone chews
they leave, Mom Mom
the children honking
the horrible geese

Glove

I couldn't get over the weather
it was like a punch
that came up from the inside
a sock to my blood
everywhere I looked
I saw trees and the wind
blowing through them
a tiny couple in dark
tables all over New York
the winter of lies

entranced in the trees
as rustness bleeds up from horizon
meeting the clouds
in her boots the saint and the
dog walk on with rock
entrenched
in a pity that laps back for ages
all the dead all the bones
the saints in their graves
the bloody balls in the
little man's mouth
& nowhere the woman
she loved, uninvented.

In the Rain

chickens spilling
over a wall, chickens
jumping like there's
a war

Twilight Train

Now the pink is in the water
its wavy edges celebrated
by cars & guys with hands
in pockets staring out. A woman
chewing gum by the window
of the train. Which heaves
its accordion on & we move.
They call it choo-choo
because of the faint chooing
sound as it starts. It's
twee too & dit dit dit
eel & screech. All this as
the colors change. The buildings
they bothered to paint
white are pink like
someone's awful socks
were mistakenly
washed. Who owns
this insidious red. The
trees are black
cause that's where the green
goes. The girl who chews
has fanned her fingers
out below the glass

and I long to stare
at them. To count
them one by one
as the wires slip
by. It's the sultriness,
the smokey approach
of the loss of
light that I love. The
homosexual lilac
comes & it's ours
& everyone like us. The
bright compartment
of white lights &
gleaming flip top &
yawns rage
on. Outside the Hudson
River queerness tools
on my brain like
a hopeless little
wallet of feeling. A clear
swipe to night. Everyone
in my compartment
is tearing now. It's true,
I heard two sheets
at once get torn
to pluck a brownie
out. Its smell
oozes, & the other

42

one, god knows
whose—to park
her gum? Her hands
are holding her
head, my silent
partner's & she's
sleeping (deep in my gaze.) I look
at her knees, the wrinkled
foot just above
the heel, a yellowish
unmoody pink. The trees
crowd the house &
finally we go fast
finally it's not so
warm on the train
& boats are sitting
on purple sand
the mountains
are bland & blue
a woman's sigh
is falling
off, from on
high and
into her body.
My partner's
knees sway.
Someone says
Proust. Or was

it Bruce. The train
is rough. Cutting
through sweetness
every night.
I think "time."
Then "cargo."

Taxing

I hate feeling
that home
is a place
where all I have
to do
is fix
things. Moving
money, shoveling
words from
one part
of the
country
to the
next,
resettling
livestock.
Big puffy
ones
that are
clearly
getting
fed differently
from the
days

when you
were the sole
approach.
I feel
sad about
what
my life
has grown
into:
a series
of bangs,
soup, all
of us do-
ing our
job in
this ancient
& lonely
way. I'm
a shepherd
that's
what I
am. Craning
my neck
so
far &
wide
the world
is empty.

There
is no
lamb.

Porn Poems

Her tongue & her
heart were
throbbing
in the holster
of her pussy.

Last Supper

It was Wednesday night &
the food was so hot
the tree sat undecorated
I watched the men
in the take out
shop, felafel men
spoon sauce generously
and I thought make
it good for me
it is my last supper.
The shape of the
little tomatoes
what is that
shape, oval
like an eye
the bottom
of the boat
a death boat
Connie pointed it out
embedded in
the architecture
of the Guggenheim
uptown, death
tucked in all

its wise corners.
I missed out
on Peggy's house
in Venice
one day
the day it was
closed. Look
through the black
gate of Peggy's
house. Hi Peggy
Dead at 138.
Can I tell you
what I ate
today? Besides
the felafel
platter I had
a bird's nest
& then, uh,
a slice and
before that
let's see am I boring
you to death?
I had a couple
of bananas, little
too ripe, bright
yellow, some
cheese & crackers
beige & blue

I had
oh I had
some banana
bread, tan.
And you know
what I thought
at the
gym tonight
I really thought
it. It was
really bright &
I was naked
I was standing
in the shower
like a mooing
cow, staring
into the
light & I
thought, life,
Peggy, life
is the only
privilege. And
the only
real toast
is food.

Eileen's Vision

One night I was home alone
quite late past eleven
and my dog was whining and
moaning and I went over
to stroke her & pat
her & proclaim
her beauty &
then I returned
to my art review
but Rosie wouldn't
stop. Something was
wrong. & then
I saw her.
It looked like a circle
a wooden mouth
in the upper third
of my bathtub
cover which
was standing
on its side
it is the Lady I thought
this perfect sphere
on the wooden
bathtub cover

incidentally separating
kitchen &
middle room
in my home
where I
live &
work. That is
all. I'm just
a simple
catholic girl
I had been
thinking, pondering
over my
review. That's
why it's
so hard
for me but the
Lady came &
she said, stay here
Eileen stay here
forever finding
the past
in the future
& the future
in the past
know that it's
always so
going round &

it is with
you when
you write

& she didn't
go, she
remains a stain
on the bathtub
cover, along with
many other stains,
the dog's leash &
half-scraped lesbian
invisibility stickers
and other less specific
but equally permanent
traces of paper &
holes four of
them and they
are round too
like the lady
& I don't have to
tell anyone.

Animal Sounds

Riding past a green
sign in a cab
doing one of those
I'm not you
speeches
in my head.
Rainy night
waited for
a bus till
2 dead ones
went by
& I gave
up. & took
you who
were friendly
who made
me write
not read
who sat quietly
with me
as the
lights streaked
the tires
sizzled

& the air
was better
than ever
on a
bus. We took
a right at
the Hotel
Cavalier
This is it right here
Loews.

Poem for My New Fortunes

I wish there were some animals
to look at animals to
watch, the framed imperceptible park
the easy trash cans are living in
some fashion, flooded with electric
light. Cabs prowl
the walls and the sounds
and the branches do nothing
that animals do. Comic facility
of their restless legs &
craning necks, the dog is always
present because she's the only
show in town. Dog discovered
squirrels this summer and birds
she sees them in the city
instead of her fellow trapped
four legged beings. Otherwise
she sits in the mud
a big juicy puddle.
She leaps on a chicken wing
I no longer feel like
a dog. Woefully human
wuffily, I hop along the beach
in a slow and slower run

and the sticky legs fellows
are fleeing and poking around
like animation their legs invented
the line and it goes like
this: tan wet warm inside
how does it feel to have hollow bones,
to be walking on tubes on the beach
covered with feathers & foam
how does it feel to be part
of the picking flock
unable to light the next
candle, your eyes, your beady
long seeking bird eyes
the place of the sun
a shower of light
gobs of it to veer through
chill air, flying in darkness
do you do that
is it a branch for a snooze
I want to see your life
not imagine it
always, your future
is done. I envy you
my legs of bone
my tiny frantic
pen that
contains me

Merk

There's too much light in my life
there that's better
the street people recommend
don't let your brother fling his
leg & arm around you like
you're his girlfriend. Humpin your
kneecap, stuff like that
the vilest smell of all tonight
is human food
it's November when the moons switch
places. White is bad
black is good. Food stinks.
Carrying their buckets of soup
to their stupid abodes
furs around their necks, beasts.
What do humans eat? Dogs, more or less.
Ripping fruit from the vine
snipping the crop
maybe vegetables would like to
let their baby be too
and never never eat the human
that is a crime. Push my machine
to see what nazi called
me. Go out and kill her with my teeth

I'm a bored outsider
the season is cold
everywhere doors are slamming
and look who you're in the
room with now. Someone to eat
I hope. Think of Goethe
Werner Goethe with his leg
flung up on a rock in
Italy. Take a bite
of that fat calf.
He's like a big posing gondola
what's the idea
every poet I know is a partial artist
the lucky ones are dead
naturally incomplete
but look at everyone you think of
hanging on to some misapprehended
particle of modernism, all
plumped up with pillows
there's nothing
after a modern idea
for poets. All they do
is think & eat. If you call
that making something
& I don't, I don't call that art.
We must offer ourselves
up as food or eat
someone. If you can make there

be less of someone else
or someone could take
a bite out of you
then you could join in the incompletion
or excess of your age
I'm sick of seeing dunces celebrated
that's the job
someone that looks
good in ribbons
someone surrounded
by their editor's
arms. Love object
of a lesbian
but not being
one. Particle board
potential screen
play, plastic
hair, translates
well, millions will hold
you on the train
bite me now
bite me forever
in your two strong

o eat me read
me something

I am the daughter
of substitution
my father fell
instead of the dresser
it was the family
joke, his death
not a suicide
but a joke

how could I accidentally
get eaten
slipping into your
sandwich or refrigerator
sort of a dick
that crawls
up from the bottom of your
ice cream cone

it's too late for some
of us, but for others
it's never late
enough. Tonight
when they moved
the lights and everything
looked completely
horrible for
a change
I was looking

for sympathy
and you asked
me for the menu

I have escaped the unseemly
death of the alcoholic
yet I keep my ear so close
to the ground & I know
what they know
I begin to smell
funny, another fate

it was as if I was falling
last night
but I imagined
myself a bit
of food
& I was safe
in your mouth
& I would
never die

it is the legacy
of my family
to change in the air
& smash as
something
new

not a woman
but a chair
full of flowers

not a poet
but a donut
or a myth

go up there
& get me a cracker
darling
& proudly
I walked

Nancy at 40

Susan Wheeler & the dead sea
scrolls! No, neither.
And he's not a poet
the voluptuous stone lion I see as Fifth
Avenue squeals. The Lion's honor &
the flag wrinkles pounding the wall for
money it comes oozing out pedalling madly
to be wrong twice so naturally my disorder
comes in pairs. No one could live
in a big city & believe
that the end of the world comes
like they said. It's a constant constant
growling, a constant request
constant monster, becoming one
shucking your horns, exposing your
softness. The last time
I thought I needed a bigger
house it took me twenty
years to realize it was small.

I think decades have shrunk
they take five years and the blood
in the eyes of the cars distracts
me from completion. Now we're like

Seattle with espresso everywhere
so I can be out of my body at home, in the middle
                                        of it.

Home is where the intelligence is & begins
I mean I have made myself something
certain actions make me strong
and there are conflicts & those
differences are an engine of
sorts, a spark
there is a tiny little body shooting through
space looking for everyone. He is my dad
sperm the message goes on &
on, there are millions of devils
in the word & they are not all men
they are more like angels, Sister,
when I hear them beep they are singing
our song. Time to get lost in the cosmos
be soft again. Is it simply a fire at home
I'm sending out a match of light
it's economical to plop me in the tub
throw in some salts & it's oh so warm
you can be here or so far away & I
can never see you again as long
as I live. But I can hear you moving around
in the room where you live
and the walls come tumbling down

66

Greek

My identity as a specialist
    behold a rotten autumn, holding
equipment, then flinging it

The dirty men begging but me
  behold I tug my dog & horrify blond
   children who will die if they
    open their mouths, my
      fist, that of a specialist
   gone out of control. The slots widen
     blasting into my day like
rat-clouds, possibilities to
     be average, yay, to be kite-tail to
      burn out, to be young again when
you're old in a metal part of town
    the river seeps and wags
   anything less I'm in a rush. Under the spot-light
Eep! the one thing I lost for sale, a buck
    on the blanket of a sleeping man. Here
   brother, I took it. Slipped the sleeping
dollar into his pocket. I touched a bum and
loved him. Thanks. A dead little story,
but I liked my hope under light. I'm sick of
film. I like things that don't move like

67

near dead men on the street. They represent
    authenticity like paintings. The woman I know
who lives outside was seen on a stoop picking
    her pimples. I mean it bothered her.
        If I can help in your education it will be
        by not showing up. Lesson Plan, big drool
sweet smile. Focus, little chips, mediating inabilities
    disgust for earnest progress. I long for a King's
        journey, from place to private place. What rose
        in me when knowledge was kicking in was shame,

                                    sentimentality
        guilt, repulsion for the quaint, heated days
in November kite-tailing, that drove me
out in possession of an animal with bloody
                thighs. I sensed I could get by
    in a squeak. Robbed on a street I walked
        down all my life. Yelling no no no
            finally Eileen Myles has
lost it in the street the children sang
    as they bought their CDs. Ripping your head
    right off. I have in utter lucidity been
obsessed with wallets. The fat cunt of
    one with all my goods inside. I stopped yet
                                    another
        poor man who works the goldfish show
    on St. Mark's. I know this is a stupid
    question but have you found a wallet.

It's not a stupid question he
        said sincerely, but if I found
    it I would have put it in there
            a church of white
people   crowded with white people
            genuflection, an occasional
            crane bursting
up through the street
        and the culture wore on.

Just God

We know the city
hates us as we
sit in our
vanilla
stained rooms.
Flick Flick. The
media ruins
our lives so we
build tunnels
in our poems
to help the
darkness in,
to give truth
to ruin, crud
to our poems.
Resist the world
resist the poem
surrender to me
today. I know something
I know love
informed by heaven
daily it's blue.
The constancy
is the thing I

love in the brownness
watch the day
harden request
to a sparrow.

Day
or jail?
Think of it perfect.
How feelable. If
this isn't heaven
what is? Inching
time. Darkness
of jacket goes
on, those
wavering
fronds. Repeating
the names of
my enemies.
Why? Is he
a prayer.
Door close.
                    She
saw the shapes
a simple shape.
It isn't
art. It helps.
Is it
clean? I'm learning

again. The day
is a window.
The day is watchful.
All we need.

■

The woods
seemed to
be falling &
in a moment
it passed

Meow Mix

Pushed the door open and nobody home
window open and the street pouring
in. Fresh. Most of his junk
gone. Juanita's brother in
a baseball cap. Arm loads of art magazines.
You know Pinky? Skinny girl, real nervous.
She shook. In that lit moment, the jazz
pouring out and the air pouring in.
Empty of its contents a life becomes
a style. Almost a setting on a knob.
The Vince moment. I closed the door,
having seen that. The particulars
crumble. Younger than me,
moved in first, fifteen
years ago. Died first.
If I've heard more footsteps. Stumble.
Fights. Popped my
dog in. I'm sorry. Juanita's carrying
a plant. Why did that live?
I don't know my family.
How would I. Living here
for fourteen years. An Austrian
girl looks at my doorway &
I walk in. Again &

again. My duty to die, I suppose.
Installing doors, painting,
finding odd little
benches in the
street. Maybe I'm moving.
Pick the furniture
up. Talk to strangers like the world
like the people
in my building. Juanita pops a box
of Meow Mix by my door. I used
to feed his cats. Dad, I'm positive.
And the next week I died. There's
his mattress on the cement. Stained,
of course. That's a life. Sure
she put it in the crook of
my doorway by mistake. Afterwards
we'll go to the beach. You can
say a few words. She winced.
I'm an alcoholic. I mean
I heard him, I said.
I mean, there may come a day
when my dog will eat
cat food.

Mr. Twenty

Everywhere I look
there's another bottle
of sparkling water
it's the new beer
new since 1978 or so.
Not so new.
Even the millennium is unspeakably silent
having been here so long
100 years of the naked emperor
is more than my eyes
can stand. His little penis
bobbing below his
big belly, his tiny toes
in small loafers.
Won't somebody stop
this man. The first thing we learned
was the world would end
in our time. Do you think
we give a shit by now
Lying at the bottom of the
toilet of the naked
emperor, every time
he flushes we're supposed
to applaud. We do not.

We yawn. That was a
really big turd the emperor
just made. Must be
for women we giggled.
Huh. I lifted my
glass to my lips
it's mostly silence now
the regular darkening
as he puts his fanny
down on the lid of the
century. It makes me just
want to do something great
for the world. If there's
another big race riot in
America I think I'll go
direct streetcar named
desire in the midst of
it. I'm sick of doing nothing
I want to help.
Naturally I'll play Stanley
an angry white lesbian
walking through the burning
streets yelling Stella
Yeah. I'm eager. I'm rubbing
my palms. No seriously
folks I was born
just a few years after the
Emperor put some big bombs

down. It was very
fertile ground. I remember
a screaming sound in the
sky but the world seemed silent
that day & then some
ashes fell, or maybe it
was a scrap of worn out
rubber from the side
of the road
somehow it fell from
the sky. It filled
with papers books
& clothes. Well how *do* I
feel about the end of
the world. He's become
beautiful to us. Look
at his color. Kind of
tawny pink. Little bits
of hair on his chest
streams of it pouring
down his legs & a
slight smile on his
thin lips. It's graceful the
way he just walks
around gazing at us
and you know why he has no
clothes. It's the ultimate
power stroke—to

show the world how you
start your morning
before they see
you, I am this
simply breast
and shoulders
forearms, slightly bulgy
waist thighs amply on
the chair, legs
crossed. Step out
& say I have no job
no interest really
in engaging, but must walk
and spin, an unclothed
lily, & you will greet
me with silence
my beforeness
my adamant
unbeginning to trample
all of you with my big ass
daily, to take that royal
ride on my own
for days and weeks till
the lie is the utter complicitude
of every living thing that
has seen me, the man,
the naked emperor
smiling at you fools. I'm

the beaming man on the motorcade
the eyes glisten
the man in the suit with
promises, my Dad,
to look into his eyes
and see myself
smiling.

The only wild thing
well we tried that for a while
some kind of truth
the only wild thing
is to complain & complain
about his nakedness
his ugly fucking naked body
marching up & down the world
making everyone pretend
to believe in him
it's more than I can
stand. I would
evacuate. But
he's everywhere.
Shitting on our heads &
our couches
children can't even see him
I mean that's a problem
Am I wrong?
It would be: in my time

there was nothing else
we gave up the fight
he was everywhere
the Sun

Me II

There's tomorrow the next can of dog food
a throat getting tighter
and the radiator chinks
eventually I love the light
every day & every night
the way it like butter slides
down the wood of
the moldings around the window
the keenness of the light
down there second street
O I am so lonely
When I grow up I take a star
and the next & the next &
the next in my rocket ship
when I grow up I gonna be
one me me me
so alone with my neck
& the hissing plumbing
you out there sniff sniff sniff
me you done me wrong
me you done me wrong
me you done me wrong
me me me me
what animal I am who

writes at night
who counts the lights
that stripe the streets
who hears the winter heat going
higher & sweeter

Needles

I seem to be left with the rest of my life
seems particularly empty & clean
with the tree gone
I imagined bundling them up
with the calendars notes and poems
I sent you
enclosing a big pound of
them (it was a big
tree) for sentiment.
The first Christmas you helped me lug
my tradition home
I watched you carefully pocket some
pine needles & I imagine
you've got a few souvenirs
of him stashed away someplace
it sickens me to be part of
a pattern. But no I swept
thousands and thousands
of green needles
down the stone stairs
of my building, the
stairs my first lover
affectionately shoved me down one night
and even as I approached

the front door
sweeping away
the first floor fags
coming in with dog
said Umm smells
good. Thought you'd like
it I quipped like any
scullery maid
and I swept my pine
needles out into
the wintery
night and the icy
sidewalk and
looked out
feeling good
& vicious. Bye.

I let the piles of needles
lying on the floor
spend the night
and the clump of
lights sat on the
orange chair
& a few ornaments
cluttered the
counter and
now they're all
gone too. I thought

about smashing
them but stuffed
them into a white
trash bag and jammed
everything into the upper
kitchen shelf some
version of trashing.
Hell I'm here.
Who were you now,
the girl who
left. Hysterically
telling the
story of her
life on and on
in the bedroom
of David's
house, way into the
night. You were
blazing. A black
lamb. Goodbye.

Remember the night
we bought the
tree and Tim
had just died.
No one understands
lesbians, but
us. The imaginary

force of girls
I tell my story
to. It was Men of Lesbos
night at WOW. Finally
a chance to be a man
lip synching at home
in front of the mirror
to an Elton John
song, Rocket Man
kind of a mating call
to you. The plan was
to be a handsome man
in a suit, but
nightly donning
my dildo and boxer
shorts, moustache
then socks tie
suit I realized
the assemblage
of the man was
the party so
I strode out
onto the stage
at WOW, and ripped
off my jeans and sweatshirt
and stood there
naked for a moment
I talked my way

through, I was funny,
and did the piece
from the bottom
up till the song
cascades and I threw
open my arms and
sang my heart
out, being joyously
unselfconsciously clothed. I cut the
song off too soon, making
that off with her
head gesture to
the girl doing
tech. You poked
your head into
the dressing
room afterwards
looking scared
as hell. You
were dating
a big nut,
but my body
looked good
right? You were scared
I would leave
my moustache
on. Oh remember
us. You sitting

on the couch. Is something
going on here, you asked.
You meant us. Yes,
I agreed. But I'm
nervous tonight
and you've got
to go home. Later
you said you got
the wrong message.
Didn't come
away knowing
I wanted you
and sat there
on the stoop.
Yes, I wanted you.
Come back to me
then, before
everything.

1993

This year is ending
fast enough
some of its branches
lying on the
street, continually
spitting, Rosie's
in heat, refrigerator's broken
stinks. Nothing's
cold. *Are you
dressing your
age?* The floor
of the platform
is spotted.
Turn. I'm not she.
The candy
splits tween
my teeth.
Fingers bloody
stumps from
picking. Even
Vogue talks
about the new
poverty. Like
Con Ed going

to incredible
lengths to
get a deposit
out of me

conversations
Ridiculous.
My dentist
says for 2000
dollars I
could fix
that smile.
Ask your publisher.
When I was a child
I wanted there
to be more
something deep
& dark in
the basement
aging. Fruits
something
sweet. Everything
shouldn't be
so quick
deep down
from the
past to
now & forward

to the
future something
is biding
its time
my wealth.
I looked
to my family
our life
is not
old enough.
My car
breaks down

I return
to my
enraged pas-
sengerhood

under a blue
& Mackerel
sky, south
on 9.
The Halloween
sky

the endearing
form of
the toilet

bowl

David Rattray
died
this year

the Last Judgment
will be based
on the weather
& earth and
how we
treat it

it's always
a burning
village

Honor has on her
land
a very
old tree

masturbating
here, in
a train
bathroom
1983

Most is
adjective
almost
is an
adverb,
that's
the difference
isn't it

no the painting
doesn't
look the
same, semi-lit
despair,
almost my
birthday
totally dark
& blades
of paler
grey—made
by the gates'
hanging geometry
around
Robert's painting
I turn
the light
on to
get this

down &
it's gone

Two father
things. One
was the
phone ringing
right
after he
died   right
after & the
woman's
voice said
is Mommy there
or Daddy
there? Um I
don't think
my mother
can come
to the phone,
there
is no
daddy.
I'll
take it
Eileen. Oh
Helen—

The only
thing that's
not broken
is me. This is
fine. This
is okay.

I
discovered
something
& then I
had to
smear it.

Gargle
with Rem-
brandt

Tim told
me lots
of keys
means
you're
going no
where
fast. I throw
one old
one into

a trash
can in
Union
Sq. Dec. 3
I feel
me surging
ahead.

Teeny rainbow
flecks
on the
floor of the
laundromat
the words
blink through
my head,
strong—

I almost
hit my
nose
on the
door of
the dryer.
He must
have
had a
"strong

Mom"

after all
that we've
been
through

the academy
of false-
ness

I hate
it here.

we need
a name
for the
homeless
a "they"
for them.

I love
it. She
only
laughs
on the
outside
it's like

she's chewing.

He in fact
is incredibly
cerebral
& I like that.

you always
pay
that's true

dicks like
fountains
fountains
of fur

grooming
is good

successful
artists
are
ordinary

I'm not
a thorough
listener
& I'm

proud
of it

up there
same gears

she laughs

the beauty
of the
ladder

spinning fan

shit, ink
on
my fingers
for the second
time, Oh that
back that
used to
bend &
thin my
waist

I like the
cracks
of action

100

you know
how it
is—she's
been
my lover.

did not surf.

a leather
glove in
each
pocket

Moshiach
is on
his way
Let's be ready
one of
those dog
laughs

Mama
someone
must drive
the cars
of the
dead

so if you
see a
red one
around
a thousand
bucks

answers
to the
name
dybbuk

O blood
dry up
on my little
black
crotch

she's a little
whore

I ally myself
with the
stern
gum chewing
black woman

spook us

evolve y'all

nova
o no
avon

at last.

you know
like when
you've
bled on
your jeans
so you
rinse
out the
crotch &
then you're
wringing it
out &
the brown
blood is
coloring
the water
& it's all
twisted
when you
squeeze

it again &
again &
it looks
like a little
dick &
you take
it to the

laundry

the dog's
on a white
rice diet
because
she has
the shits
& you're
44 today

& you have
to go to
Baruch this
morning to
teach the
conditional

then visit
Joe &

104

see Nicole's
art & nap
& meet
Jennifer

we could
agree
on that

soon it'll just be
me & Hilly
fate's
fat men

in the
country
of the
young audience

one door
ajar to
the yard
& it's small lit
rectangle
is thrown
on the floor
so is the
door and

the wide
bright frame
of light

prose fills
the window
& becomes
abstract
however

think about
once the
poet stood
& the words
were in
her mind &
she stood
in inspiration's
doorway
speaking
that was
a poem

I was
so old
& it was
so over

old barking
tree people

it's 82
in my
room

what's great
is that
the fashions
change
but the
paintings
don't
in those
outdoor
art shows
boats nudes
trees

the media
lets people
know they're
not isolated
it's like
god
they thought
it was just

their little
isolated
opinion
& learn
no, a lot
of people
feel that
way

god is like
a lot &
a lot of
people want
god &
jump on
to things
that way
as soon
as they
know that
god sees
it they
want it
a lot

anything
disposable
you're bound

to soon
have too
many
of

the virtues
of stillness

now that we're
through
with virtual
reality
we can
try virtue
it might
work

I hold
the tree
still while
you clip
the branches
you call
this butch

getting
a tony
hold

your head
still

funny
to see
the flag
out there
like a
porkchop

my flag.

The intelligence
of it
all
that loop
of branch
hanging
like a halo
of the end
of year

one jabbing
branch still
with brown
leaves like
scarves
the birds

carrying
the message
flapping
about

I have
in front
of me
an enclosure
for a view

for nearly
20 years
reading these
bricks &
branches
like a tea-
cup apart
from the
squalling
rest of
the world
whoops &
I see this
death from
year to year
flossy with
leaves bare

green
a soup
bowl
of imprecision
it really tells
you nothing
but prepares
you to go
or not

it is the art
in my
eye

my father
who was
no longer
beautiful
shocked
me as
I was
walking
down
the street

the dark
floating

of boats

want sex
want deep
deep sex
desire
performing

I love
our watches
by the
tub

some of us
just lived
our lives
faster to
avoid being
eaten

dinosaurs
invented
flowers

is that flash?

don't worry
I've got

another &

the history
channel
it's evening
in the
future

we now return
to dinosaurs

feel the
cold whooo
hurry up
to the
houses

They really
have mastered
the art
of puppetry
whatever
you call
it

Better by far you
should forget and
smile than that

you should remember
and be sad

the pseudo value
& the real value

Say for instance
the pseudo value
is the content
or the meaning

the real value
is the machinery
power, money

we care less &
less about
the first
or now
the real value
eats everything
it just
does, it's the

style of
business
today

the drugs
went into
the bicycle
that's where
the drugs
went

I like Friday's
edge

In my
deep passivity
I'm the
stalker

Don't they
know I
said
everything?

No guides.

This meeting
shot its
wad
early

yawn

He's one
of those
people I'm glad
I'm not
involved
with

his voice
is low

once there
was a
moment
when I
fell down
on the
way to
school
they thought
I had
polio
maybe
I remember
when I
fell
the collapse

I was standing

in the
doctor's office
with my
mom

and everything
was white

I was
a little
naked
girl

the doctor
said
walk over

there
towards

the window

this was
for everybody

& I
was

five.

the skill
after years
of practice

of watching
the lines
of light
grow absent
& fuller

as the
train approaches

I'm late

I thought it
said dark
psychotherapy

it said
park.

There it
goes.
a big

blanket
of food
the last
year of
the day
no, I mean

The Lesbian Poet

The Lesbian Poet[1]

I've given talks about being a presidential candidate, and a talk about being a poet in the world, which was essentially the same talk, and once I addressed being a lesbian on a panel called From Pop to Porn. I was on a panel about Censorship and Acid Migration in books, I was on a panel called Shakespeare's Sisters, I was on a panel called I think marginalization, representation and the sub-culture of queer. I don't think I've ever addressed exactly the twin topics of lesbianism and poetry which is kind of the area I've been invited to address. Ed[2] said it was something about the area of feminism, gay or lesbian issues, something like that, that tradition. I drew a figure in my notebook, three circles that joined at one point, and lunged at it—that's it, my spot, but then I realized it was poetry or the poetics of it that I was needing to address and I've hardly been anywhere other and I want to honor the place that I stand. I have to say it's literally the poetry project, St. Mark's church that I'm talking about—I came out here as a poet and a dyke maybe all in one reading. I read with Joe Ceravolo in 1977 and I read my love poems to a woman, Rose, and it seemed that I was everything, all at once, after that. It wasn't that I wasn't a poet before that, but I'm addressing some kind of surge, a moving forward that happens at some points in a poet's life, so I

---

1. "The Lesbian Poet" is a talk I read at St. Mark's Poetry Project in May of 1994 as part of the Revolutionary Poetry Symposium.
2. Ed Friedman, Director of St. Mark's.

mean I was all there, body and soul after that. I think we all write our poems with our metabolism, our sexuality, for me a poem has always been an imagined body of a sort, getting that down in time, it moves this way and that, it is full of its own sense of possibility.

I was making my marks. I think we need to line poetry up with all the other arts. We are simply making marks, marks of sound, marks on paper. We are notating our own mortality. My friend David Rattray died last spring and I went out to visit him several times in Amagansett, a beautiful place to die. He was a person who talked constantly and during his waning months I would often whip out a notebook to get down what he said. This is the same guy I had devised a signal with, earlier in our friendship. We were riding on a train and I would lift my hand at various points in his monologue which meant he should stop. I couldn't breathe. He was talking that much. One day sitting in his house I told him how when I was a dieting nineteen-year-old in Boston I would close my eyes and see the day as an empty page with horizontal stripes which represented meals. David said that's interesting because the first writing occurred in Egypt, and the parchment represented the Nile and its first use was to indicate future shipments of food and how much. Rafts and rafts of the stuff. Poetry, not prose.

It indicates desire. My poem is a menu.

My girlfriend just called and she's in a restaurant with friends and do I want to come by. First Avenue and 10th. Sapporo East. I go shooting forward sitting right here. I don't go. I know that she wants me.

Last summer I was standing alone on a hill with my dog and a car as an amazing shower of meteorites *flash*

flash had stained the sky orange. It was so sensational and I was utterly alone with my animal. I knew I was a man. It was utterly clear, there was no thing of woman at all. I was standing in nature alone, this guy. It was a terrifically human feeling. Alone. Completely full.

I would watch the birds and the water and the trees. I was only notation. Now a glob of purple lilacs is dunking over my power book which is perched on a huge dictionary. The building I've lived in for seventeen years has walls like skin. Its doors and footsteps, loud Chinese spoken in the hallway, piano music have pierced my poems again and again. Its pipes, phones, newscasters are writing my poems. There's no plaque on the outside of 86 E. 3rd. I'm not dead. My poem is a plaque of all of them, their moving, its inside. Boom. Another door slams. Monumental Wednesday.

A lesbian is just an idea. An aesthetic one perhaps. Hugh Kenner explains that Sappho is the standard for each poetic age and like David's parchment thesis, it may not be true, but I buy it. I trot it out in workshops all the time. We have so little of her, quotes existing in someone else's poems or those ratty pieces of parchment riddled with holes, "I burn *blank blank blank*." Swinburne said you should fill in the holes, "I burn *incredible lilacs in a big heaping shaking blaze*." Mr. Longline. Pound aestheticized the absence. Which also seems too precious a thought, but that's modernism—swinging quietly in the breeze of the death machine. John Ashbery said, I would put it all in, then I would take it all out. He never made up his mind. I don't think he really needed to, evolving a style that took his wavering into account.

Painters taught me to look at the edges, that's when

you aestheticize, when you get to the edge. In the poem you're turning around. The flickering lights of the fading lines re-erupting one quarter inch down, unpredictable, rude. She hopes to give the impression it's barely been mined this mineral being, yet it shines like prophecy itself, an accident. Sentence chips, poetry fading into prose, hunks of it waning. Making Frankenstein with our lips. He's laughing at what I wrote. You said she has a really big cunt. Isn't that the worst thing he shrieks. It's an insult. You know they like it tight. Isn't that why men leave their wives after they've had babies. Suddenly he's looking up a hole. But, it's different for us. We love it. Huge with desire. An incredible dripping cave.

Edmund White states in *Esquire* that there's no real culture in America now. That's why he lives in Europe. What with AIDS and "Kamikaze feminism." To Ed we are dead, we women, with our zany demands. As a literary lesbian vis à vis gay men I'm more alone than ever before. The awesome mortality AIDS conjures up leaves fags ever more protective of their lineage. Melvin Dixon pleading at the 1992 Outwrite conference in Boston, "Who will call my name when I'm gone." We will, I whisper but I've never been so aware of the conversation between lesbians and gay men, not going on. Men want to be remembered by men. When a man dies, it's the need to be valued by men, not women, that counts. History, and we still know who keeps that.

When I teach workshops I've always brought in both women and men, poetic models, but actually I've got many more fathers. I was writing poems, like I said, before I came out and wanted to get ahead, to know what you had to know to be in the conversation. It was mostly

126

men who were doing the talking. For many years my favorite poets were Jimmy Schuyler, John Wieners and Robert Creeley. My three favorite living poets, I'd emphasize and was proud that I had met them, they had signed my books and with one I was actually friends, Jimmy, and the other two—Creeley, I know him and John Wieners I always see him in Filene's basement or catching a smoke on a rainy day under the roof of the Harvard Coop. Hi John, I go. Yeah, yeah, yeah, he says, talking softly. I think he's my uncle, my uncle John. Where's the mothers. Gertrude, Gertrude Stein, of course. And all the living women I know.[3] Recently I began claiming men, a new idea. To not be ashamed of their influence on me, who was undoubtedly female, lesbian. I began demanding

---

3. I guess I could name a few. Danine Ricereto, Alice Notley, Deborah Weinstein, Camille Roy, Rae Armantrout, Tracie Morris, Kellie Cogswell, Joan Larkin, Michelle Tea, Lee Ann Brown, Leslie Scalapino, Karin Cook, Sapphire, Kristin Stuart, Carla Harryman, Shannon Ebner, Bernadette Mayer, Susan Wheeler, Jan Heller Levi, Ann Rower, Cecilia Dougherty, Brenda Coultas, Lyn Hejinian, Stephanie Grant, Susan Howe, Maggie Nelson, Cynthia Nelson, Dodie Bellamy, Jennifer Blowdryer, Mary Beth Caschetta, Elaine Equi, Tom Carey, Diane DiPrima, Eliza Galaher, Jennie Portnow, Tory Dent, Barbara Barg, Honor Moore, Ann D'Adesky, Lucia Berlin, Harryette Mullen, Kathe Izzo, Jane King, Barbara Guest, Heather Lewis, Jill Johnston, Linda Smukler, Lynn Tillman, Madeleine Olnek, Rose Lesniak, Bea Gates, Ann Lauterbach, Amy Gerstler, Holly Hughes, Gerry Pearlberg, Myra Mniewski, Laurie Weeks, Robyn Selman, Kathy Acker, Anne Waldman, Sarah Messer, Josie McKee, Elinor Nauen, Susie Timmons, Adrienne Rich... (actually you can pick up a copy of *The New Fuck You / adventures in lesbian reading* [Semiotext(e), 1995] edited by Liz Kotz and myself)... Marilyn Hacker, Maggie Estep, Erica Hunt, Lori Lubeski, Gail Scott...

my lineage, if I felt I had it. I brought almost solely their poems in. That quiet poem by Allen Ginsberg in *Howl*— "Transcription of Organ Music." "I remember when I first got laid, H.P. graciously took my cherry, I sat on the docks of Provincetown, age 23, joyful elevated in hope with the Father, the door to the womb was open to admit me if I wished to enter." "I Know a Man"—"As I sd to my friend, because I am/always talking, John, I/sd, which was not his/name…" Jimmy Schuyler counting counting then looking up at the sky in a quiet explosion. Pretty ejaculatory. I have to say I began to perceive a male shape, a conversation with God the Father. A conversation man to man, because of course I am not alone in my mortality, men are also making marks. And showing their marks like a man. Masturbating, having sex with God. It strikes me that the act of creativity, male creativity is a conversation with a masculine God, a self-fulfilling act of male conception, something roomy. I know that I can't see like a man, fuck like a man, not exactly. His literature doesn't fit me. Nor should it. He makes art for different reasons from me. To perpetuate himself. To rewrite woman.

------

4. Rather than fool with the talk I gave at St. Mark's, I've decided to footnote some of my meanings. When I talk of "unwriting" myself, I'm thinking of it as the act of shedding. You can put on your mother's clothes, or you can take them off, but you're still her daughter. It's a performance of being that I'm after. Being female of course means something different to women than it does to men. It's a given that I'm alive, so I don't have to be "conceived" again. To stand in that place more firmly, though, I find myself consciously breathing *out*, exhaling, unwriting, so to speak. The huge fact of my body has all the momentum of literature. When I'm dead I'll have shed a lot. I leave it to girls *and* boys.

If I were to start unwriting[4] myself, Eileen Myles, I would begin with my name. That's the title of the poem, I own her. When I came out I felt that philosophically I could jump off the wheel, that being a lesbian meant not giving birth, that the buck would stop with me and I liked that. My parents were post World War II working class Bostonians who it seemed did not achieve many of their dreams or ambitions, and me deciding not once but many times not to reproduce would keep my sights upon the horizon of my own life, a bold and egocentric move, I felt. Since then of course being a lesbian has proved to have nothing to do with childlessness—many of my friends have dug up some sperm and gone ahead so it's a personal decision it seems, a female one and not related to my lesbianity. This is so heavy. I want to throw this damn speech away. I want to say something else about my femaleness, which is what interests me, not feminism. Femaleness is owning my woman's insides.

In a culture wild about dick it's essential, I think, to do some kind of owning, of what's inside your belly, the invisible. Your private use of your ovaries, uterus—I don't mean your pussy, your clit, the things that everyone values when they're citing our sex. All you need to do is hit your thirties and meet some male gynecologist or female, they went to the same school, who wants to yank your uterus out, just for the fun of it, and it never occurs

---

We know what rewriting means, it occurs *on* something you're not. The problem is that men don't think they're women. If they came out of the sky they'd be rewriting that. Admittedly, it's difficult to be here for all humans. That's why we write at all. We're shedding thinking. More men ought to start unwriting themselves. Soon.

129

to him that this is castration, or that a small discharge leaking out of the tip of his dick would *ever* cause a doctor to calmly suggest we might cut off his balls. I began a practice of naming, owning, praying after that, liking every node and tube and squeaky tunnel in my female belly. I want it there, it's mine. My poem rumbles through it all, unbelievable, and as the month turns the poems get manic, crazy, weird, sullen and bloody, stay at home, the words I use narrate a female cycle, probably much more than a female orgasm.

When I came out as a Lesbian poet I named my first book *Sappho's Boat*. Very definitely because my earlier book's content was half in and out and a bookstore called Oscar Wilde wouldn't carry it because it wasn't gay enough. I wanted to be in the store. You want gay, here's *Sappho's Boat*. I feel self-conscious about lesbian things, in nature like I said I'm nobody, this human, a man. I claim my femaleness, first if you want take it from me, any of it, my dark possessions. It's my poetic dilemma, it seems. To include the body, mine, the woman's as I see it, to approach this blood as part of the score. It should show up regularly in the culture's poems, this female conversation, because most of the poets who write bleed every month until they pass childbearing years. I'm waiting to watch the room change.

There is a word in Italian, *affidamento*, which describes a relationship of trust between two women, in which the younger asks the elder to help her obtain something she desires.

Women I know are turning around to see if that woman is here. The woman turning, that's the revolution. The room is gigantic, the woman is here.

My man, Ed White, wrote an article in *The New York Times* about gay fiction. The woman he mentioned was Gertrude Stein. It's a pity she's dead. Yet the fact that our century's greatest poet is a lesbian is nothing to sneeze at. That her work can be seen as clicking with the rhythms of a female body, and she looked like a man, *what a butch*, is fine. She studied circulation, the circulation in the human body, in college, it's wonderful. That she was a student of William James and stands in the line with Emerson and Thoreau is cool. Is radiant with the undercurrency in American literature that assures us that the moment of being is central and true. That a woman, unwriting herself, flooding the world with her details, standing in such an endangered place could be free.

2

Kurt

The weekend you died was
really a big deal for both
of us. You were really
cute, and such a brilliant writer,
and so fucked up. It was
like seeing our insides
on the screen of MTV
that weekend, being famous.
All your songs seemed
special to me after
that. I never knew
how to claim them
before. The raspiness
in your voice was
real, we stayed up all night
watching the same
pink videos
of you on unplugged
seeming tremendously
sad, and now dead.
Your death was something

we could share. We read
every single article
we could get our hands
on, Circus, Rolling Stone,
anything. I felt I knew
it all—about Kurt and when
I was done I would
hand him to you.
I guess it was great that there
was something we both
loved, this dead guy.

Aurora

I come from a long line of worshippers of strong crazy
    women
I have been holding you
walking along the clouds that hover over the Neva
and as each screaming teakettle arrives
at a point that's clean of disease,
the moment boiled away
and as the red velvet curtain whisked
to either side
down seams of cruelty you cried
I kept sweeping you clean of meaning
and light

in Mockba
as each pedestal of the worker glistens as the trains
vanish every fifty seconds
LED agree
and spinning chandeliers of imperiality meet waning
soviation and incremental candy bar express
is on its way and the middle
range is absent. It's either the very old and singular

way too pricey, shiny stuff, or a commonplace that
    can't be
lifted easily and in between it's
gone that's why we're here. Pushing palms
against the columns, fists of empty blue cans of gin
averring snickers and vouching for pelmany
huge moon water, voda, Da Da.

At the font of your resolution to stuff a rug in a bag
make too late dinners for no one
in the weakness & the wentness
I have been holding you
in the gentle tomboy's tears
zipping sounds, success! Only a river could take you
    home

zharka boots, having utterly no interest in
    Dostoyevsky's
being open to instant messages
being a brick in the family pattern
long ranging flight pattern
understanding vertigo but not now

realizing to take the picture

138

I know what gerunds are
crying through dinner very satisfying
know what else?
I know the cups you wanted were
a loving cup of lying there forever
on that train.

How I Lost My Notebook

Quietly wishing I
had testicles

lost 3

what were the
other two

a heaving
hole & the
second roommate
observed
me, it slipping
out

plop
my chipmunk
on the ground
protect my rage
by being minor

tick tick

I tossed that

cylinder
of red &
green on
the floor

like Sarah Schulman

even the wind shift

& a tiny

stop writing

Trill yes of
black smoke

my exile
in America

oh help me
I need my
glasses all
the time

exiled by
age

into a cylinder
of observation

& brutal
remarks

upon the plain
we saw a
twister coming

I've been here before
the tattersall
curtains

our violent dish

I mean I must
leave but

I might
die

wet is bad enough
coffee, whatever
fluid

not the grinder

it's the
first said
the intern
chuckling

use the protector
no virgin births

we've had a few

I said no virgin
births

my sun is not Jesus
my brother was not
Jesus
my father was
not Jesus
nor you
doctor

nor all the
men in the
telephone book
hanging in
the booths
in new york

we nameless
start saving
the kids
in their 40s

the female ones
throw them
on the boat

whatever the song
when the
boat went
down forever
singing in the
water

whatever the
song and
its variants

I am in a hospital
now be Frank

I'm here for help
the city possesses
all different kinds
of services
some survive

144

some don't

if I see a bird
I know there's
land

unless the bird
is very very tired
in which case
I attach
this note

The City

It's narrow
down here
a small
turn can
be very
wrong.

the female voice
is the sound
of the future
don't you
think

Modulated
& the door
close softly
it is 4 o'clock

An Explanation

I have this compulsion to live no matter what
that's why I did what I just did
yet everything in the universe seems sad
eat a banana
plastic jars of laxative
my lap-top's gong
it's good to be so clear for once
I have no interest in the gaining media access
panel. At exactly 2:30
it's where I'll precisely not be
I imagine, I understand a world based on positive
      inactions
a glossy don't
a fervent won't
if for a second I dread carrying the lug of my
      corporeality
up the stairs, I think of sex or something like it
not being dead and it's that as well as my books
and socks and computer, battered knees
and twisted ankles I swing over the shoulder
of something strong up the 26 steps.
So now, having arrived home, having traversed
an ocean of stone, New York, to be in the cozy home
of a simple idiot. To make a cup of coffee, black
and strong, to be here in the early November
afternoon and the drapes of the individual
leaves are charming, like earrings, are like
torn gloves on my good old tree. I have nothing more
to offer you but stripes of light.

Greetings

Sad
New England
the baseball
fields & the
grey everywhere
waiting for god.
He is in the rain
the New York signs
that decorate her
train stations
Tell me some more

Trees bricks
sad rules
the beamy
eyes of
cars. A river
with a bridge
& rickety
houses, wooden
porches. Mom.

Christmas

Susie said Morton has an island right between Haiti
& Cuba, really close
Morton Salt, they have a big factory there, on this little
    island
and that's all there is. 1200 people live on that island
and they all work for Morton. You should see the
big salt pans it's just like these big lakes
and they dry up and there's all this salt.
That's where it comes from.
On the rest of the island there's a wildlife
preserve. And on the other side
from Morton there's a coral reef. It's a fossil coral reef
so you can imagine. It was really hot,
it was not like a vacation over Christmas
imagine it in the hot sun
it was gruelling. Tim, the egomaniac,
the young twenty-year-old, a nice girl,
and the Good guy, what was his name *Mel*.
There wasn't a spot for a woman of her age
on this particular expedition,
I mean they couldn't tell stories

and she would go *Oh*, and she wasn't a specialist
like Ruth Ann Biddle, bigger than the
guys and it seems you have to be bigger
or smaller than them or else you just vanish
bungling alone. It's all how they hate women,
I said. They hate us so much that there
are like four roles, like statues,
and they can't see you if you're anything else.
We agreed, had lost our innocence, one does,
and now we just wanted power and peace.
There was a guy on the plane back,
a businessman, just a regular guy
and he was explaining, oh I don't
know something about human relationships,
in the work place. Just that there was
such a thing, Susie said, was really nice.
She had been at work,
not on a tropical island.
Susie said, one day when they were
walking to work, there were thousands
of shoes and pieces of clothes washed
up on the beach. He sold insurance, but he was really
        human.
He was a nice man, she stated. I sighed.

150

Can I tell you more about my breakup?
Sure, she said. You've been listening
to me.

White Orchids

What kind of
flowers
are these
in the pot?
The spill
looks accidental
upon their
chest & eyes
a splash
of deepest
maroon
a splatter,
delicacy
that
contains
the wound
& go on
with open eyes

Limbo

There was a party I was at about 10 years ago. It was the first time I got the 80s look. It was all around me—neat young guys with their hair carefully cropped around their ears. Ears were kind of 80s. Girls wore red lipstick and dressed and really looked like girls. It was scary. Ten years have passed and most of those guys are dead. Now they have longer hair and smoke cigarettes and everyone it seems wears glasses. It's a smart look. Despite the earrings and the tattoos they look like college students. Now I'm mainly seeing that they're young. I like this privacy. They pat my dog and read carefully, smoking away. I come up to the counter several times a day, everytime I come to this cafe and say what's that tape. They say something 70s the past, their eyes glint and gleam. I don't remember it exactly like this. Something of mine, now yours, a song blowing through an open cafe and it's young. The eyes wide open, the colors strong. Remember that boy that everyone loved, Mark Dumay.

Spaceless

There's no kind of care
that could make the space
I've created
be of any
use

it's in the future now
to be considered
fraught & spot

to be pathetic,
wide open
my ribs
twisted
like my sneakers

divorced between
quality &
community
the legions of udders
assembled
stuff
sitting on its
checkerboard

I'm lonely now
an improbable
disassembled
something on
a chair

under a moon
dead something
disconnected
something else
don't care
everlast outbreak
the batteries
be precise
asteroids don't do it.
Kid stuff,
foreign countries,
language
tits, no
sex don't
cars die
buildings all
wrong
my schedule
inevitable
salt 'n pepper
please. Who
won?

Odalisk

A toe points at me
I don't know you
your face is a mask
it holds too long
I wait for a wrinkle
your inscrutable
beauty
what's going on
I really can't draw
all the years I've thought of
you
Big Lion
sort of an L
inside by a gate
where I lie
a tiny diamond
all my sorrow
collides in a flash
of sun
inevitably I'm climbing
in. You want me home
I can tell by your
wail
it's like the day I

was done
everytime I hear
you cry
I'm getting out again
in some moment
I will cease
it will be like everything
before
you bring me that much
joy, my vanishing moments
I fall in
a yawn & everything
white, a slimy
little shudder
it ceases
I walk the world
baby I sing your song
setting still
a teeny ray of light
just as night
begins
shoulders, crotch
nipple &
hand I would
tear the world
wide open
just to live
in your cave

& the light
goes down
I shut me
tight. For you
to be born
again. Breathing
you make
everything
wake.

True North

I want to be
the invisible
man. As he
tears through
the streets
his shape
in the
snow

it seems
my relationship
to history
is not
a particular
thing.

It's no easier
in the sun.

Throttle you.
It's a letter
between Y &

tee. It's where

the vowels
go. She
wanted to
have sex

for at least
10 years.

She wanted
to kill
me.

Mom.

If I was
just her
son.

The Poet.

His moves in
the snow.

Do you think
I'm a man?

Sometimes I
just have to

make great
art.

my grandma
with a
knife

she said
John
get a
job.

Least
she cared.

everything
in front of
me is connected
to everything
else in
front

brush my teeth
& don't
bite

I was not
Hannibal Lecter

nice motel

cool, relaxed

I'm insulted
by the
shape of
the skirt
on the
door

Is that my
Twat?

If I am
not a
man

how could
I be so
incredibly
important

snow so
white coming
down

shovel, shovel

Beam.

With these
I could
build a
culture

ask my wife

He's right
she said

he's the
builder
I'm all mind

looking out.
the street
looks clean

my grandma
went mad

trying to get
something
out of him

I quit.

I'm moving
around.

The problem
is I am
not a star
inside of
life

I am something
warm (a figure)

melting snow.

A Poem

A woman is ugly   she
becomes her mask
a hyena a thin word
shaking sneer why don't
you get em
on the speaker phone
all your *friends*
She whines   NO I shout
she trembles squeals
I'm killing her   NO
I will not shut up   SLAM
why don't you get
em the speaker phone
when you are calm
Fuck you! I will never
be calm again, breast
full of circling
anger. Hole
she spouted
white fire from.
Uncorked. The night they
went back.

Gold

Moon or mouse?
And in the pain of frosted
mirror, you dance
a pink blur

and if every Friday
was just like this
afternoon, a long
breezy layover
watching the privileged
child, long brown
hair in her
backyard
up the blood slide &
down some
clit
explode it seems
like everything's veiny
in Minneapolis
of drip-free
future hoops, thy swinging
house for birds.

The
higher passed
in a weary wave
of Lilac it seems
so many hours
ago I heard the
coffee come

The yards
are connected
on & on *I'm hurt*
I said in the fireplace
lounge & a man
profiteth

the girls shake
their heads
I change everyone's
lives by being
inky let her whistle,
wait in silence
No more.
O sit with it. The long
haired girl running
beautiful legs, continuous
yards to St. Paul
Omaha, to you?
It's all too much.

I'm nobody's
slave, so

meet me.
in the middle
when I noticed
the girls go
home & eat
some lunch. The
trees are empty
soon full.

The rights of man
are invisible if
not interconnected
like the yards
in which I
reach for
you in pain
& bliss
& total disregard
the water boils!

shit I sound like Adrienne
rich the kid
returns. A certain
amount of tender
dwelling heals

the wyrdest wounds.
Two girls

now she slides
the pole,
bigger one
black, she pulls
the ropes

I dream in
disregard
through a fuzzy
gauze of
April trees.

Woo

Out in a bus stop
among the
mountains
a yawn, boy drive by
blue mountains
little tan mountain
house, similar
each scape
is all its own place
no woman
is like any
other

At a Waterfall, Reykjavik

I still feel like
the world
is a piece
of bread

I'm holding
out half
to you.

Rotting Symbols

Soon I shall take more
I will get more light
and I'll know what I think
about that

Driving down Second Ave. in a car
the frieze of my hand
like a grandmother
captured in an institution
I know I'll never live here again etc.
many many long years ago
Millions of peeps in the scrawl
the regular trees
the regular dog snort &
dig. In the West Village
you could put on a hat
a silly hat & it's clear
whereas over here
20 years passed
that rotting hat
it's loyalty to someone or something
that's really so gone
the moment clenched
like religion or government.

Wait a minute. I prefer
umm a beatle's cap
when it's really really old
neighborhood devoted to that.

Poetry is a sentimental act
everything spring she said
being surrounded by so much rot.
Pages & pages
mounds of them that I'm in
not some library but in your
little home, like you.
Every season I know I'm leaving
I'm as loyal as the cross
to this smeltering eccentricity
down by the river with Daddio
toss your ball in the river
in the future over bridges
they say you have to imagine
the 20th century. *All these buildings were*
        colored
a blasted interior
scarlet curtains rattling day
cobwebs on inexplicable machinery
a theater once dwelled here
all I see is rotting ideas
the epics I imagined
the unified cast of everyone

eating turkey together
on a stage
my idea
like waters towers popping up
feeling mellow
not exactly nothing all this time
but the buildings that are absolute
gone that I never
described. You can't kill
a poet. We just get erased &
written on. It aches in
my brain, my back
this beauty I'm eating my toast
everyone I knew you would
be dead tomorrow
& *you were*. The composing camera
infatuated with the shovel
on the lid & the pile
of rocks. He is not aging
same Alexandrian
blond in Bini-bons
the sirens are gods
when I lifted my head
from my swarming difficulty
You were so marvelous
bringing those toys to my feet
in between the invisibility of
the constant production & consumption

the network of that
& apart from the mold.
You survived.

Bob Dylan

for Shannon Ebner

I can't taste my pie
this mood goes elsewhere
past my dirty hands
like a noodle to a spring
teeny weeny bites
I'm like a big yelp
ulp Hello
my lines look all wrong
if this is the way
I'm flung
into history
Here is my house.

Absolutely Earth

I like movies because
I get to look
at other people
it's so lonely at night
there aren't many movies
about swans
or buildings
though I saw one where a building
kept coming back
a little square red one
well actually
it was a hospital
a haunted one
kept coming around
a movie's like a solar system
three slow planets maybe four
urging toward inevitability
a plot in a car
the foot of the dead man
sticking out on a hill
and the music swells
I thought this is like
my love life
all at once I get

it and it's really too
much
you could see it coming
& then it went
the shit hit the fan
through a little
trap door
on the floor
just look at all these
people on my
screen

Mom

The youngness
of these flowers
withered
they barely speak
as if youth had
more to say
with its head held
up. Their microphone's
down, these lilacs.
Yet I remember
swan place
so rich in them
streaming down
the street
I think of you
when the
flowers were
new
I lived
in your
house.

Sullivan's Brain

If there's a person in the paintings
say a boy and a dog on the beach
they call it narrative
no cute jokes
the head is talking now
you can name a cloud in Latin
you can name a wind
in Shakespeare
when "it" soliloquizes
do we turn & whisper
bill speaks
I like the crunch of
Rosie's jaw on
science diet
the caw of her
throat but
my language tends
to personalize
in the Rain
dog's name
the name of the product
it contains
the ker-clump
"I must go out"

Peepers attend
the newly configured yard
where a tree fell
down & lies there
& a virgin who observed
my coming out
just stares & creeps
say whatever's peeping
out. Its beauty is
beyond me. I start
backing my car up
you girls & your structuralism
post haste have taught
me so much. The angry
dog shaking shaking
the metonymic
bird. Not daughter
but slaughter.
I left the ghetto
I'm standing way out
the black & the prongs of light
surrounding me
doodling in Nature
There is no one
on my beach
normality is a dot
morphing away
every single cunt

began to feel like a movie
the cameras are rolling,
Love. To stay here
or there.
I like,
No I can't
say that.

In the sickest
morning I ever
saw a structure, a totem
growing in your tiny
house, a green
thing, the smile
of arousal
like an em-dash of a beach
it's too easy for you
to be pretty I tell them
we all know birds
squeak & cry

Wiggly
describes my
desire, an
aesthetic
if we imagine a light source
somewhere & all the
leaves living &

the dead can be said
to be moving
before its big
loud eye
then we move
towards living in art
interfacing in awe
not orgasm
but is one
yes but don't touch me again
I'm done. Finally the
dog settles down
I know rugs says bill
it's about threads I suppose
counting them

her half hour
stretches so long
on a day like today
the radio at large
no beach
walking
up the steps
to my abstraction

My War is Love

I was moved
something that didn't happen in sex
happened in my eyes
I feel like some old veteran
you left your marks on me
I could feel the concessions
brewing storm clouds
in the distance
upstate New York & its stabbing
vistas
you can see the man who knew
so much had a lousy house
Thomas Cole
the other one had insurance
money
it makes a difference
you know Hartford, '91,
but nothing can protect us
from heartbreak
like weather
the death of a child
we walked through
their house
spotting views

As you move through
the house at
the sculpted trees
it was only death in their eyes
I think of the past that way
upstate New York
these men's big mansions
a little baby grave
I think of my love as a dead child
cunt like the barrel
of a gun
scraping myself against you
the words are gone
I'm watching my love grow
invisible
both my parents had
these tiny children
sisters & brothers
we never knew
every veronica makes me sad
a baby's grave is
like a little belly
baby graves in my eyes
if the most innocent
victims of a war

loved, most invisible
the pig won

and that makes me glad
the farmer had to dance
& the animals watched
but the pig had to sip
sip and survive
the pig in a house
I think about walking
in these houses
with you
that once upon a time
you would know that the sun
set there &
we had a river
the battle is lost I sob
in the middle of war
they twirled the house
round & round in
their heads
he died when the century
was one
each window was a perfectly
imagined day
when it rained the eyes cried
battered by weather
so many days
empty the trees &
the eyes see far
all the maroon fortunes

of the churches
the precious little family
like a life in a box
I was haunted by views
something that the rich
leave to be
sit down & smile around
the flapping of days
the windows close
and the day turns in
we light a lamp
in our eyes

Story

About a poet
you might
say—he's really
good at
being alone.
You might lie
low with your
head hanging
down
or look up at a shirt
on a door
that smells of her
& say she's gone
you might cry
either way
but one feels
better. I don't see
it that way, she said
on the phone
it's the truth
I said
I'm vanishing.

Waterfall

I miss whiskey
regular fun
meet a girl
know I'd won

I miss whiskey
what a dope
now I'm sober
horny,
broke

Whisky I miss
you, I had
a friend
you're never alone
with an elbow
to bend

I play a guitar
but music stinks
I sit in nature
typical oinks

typical bahs, neighs

& whinny
typical doodle
bloooo
ka-thunk
ka-thunk

In me speaks
the divine
menagerie
the nectar
the blood on my hands

Girls Girls Girls!
I came to pray

Tonight

Just for the fuck of it
my arms are stripes
I fling them upwards
to be part of it, trees
to be one with all the things
in the world, sap,
rockets going up.

I'm pink & shiny round
a pale face
I'm a pearl, hear my
silence in the ponds
of the world, see my name
come dripping
out of my mouth like fish
drip out from my circle

Hey just for once
I felt the thing rising
in the rockets of my
fame, to pull in the limbs
my roots, quit the community
find my sandals
walk, save my self

millions of candles know our
distance, flower magic
hits of light dropping
down the trees of my game
everywhere is a kind of travel
every distance is me, you, when I go

in the woods a deer is moving
call me crunchy leaves
starry night, Mammy,
the ringing sounds of your hoofs
in the light in the woods
Tonight.

No No

Look I don't know
about getting
things back
a woman stands
in a room
& it's winter
she sees herself
there are 3 hot things
to tell her lover
soon the day
changes shape
not this bird
but it's different
the box stays
the room in her head
soon both heat
& winter are gone
I want to live
in my thoughts
of you, I believe
in you like a door
that returns

Printed May 1997 in Santa Barbara
& Ann Arbor for the Black Sparrow Press by
Mackintosh Typography & Edwards Brothers Inc.
Text set in Sabon by Words Worth.
Design by Barbara Martin.
This first edition is published in paper wrappers;
there are 200 hardcover trade copies;
100 hardcover copies have been numbered &
signed by the author; & 20 copies lettered
A-T have been handbound in boards by
Earle Gray & signed by the author.

PHOTO CREDIT: Dona McAdams

EILEEN MYLES was born in Cambridge, Mass. in 1949, was educated in Catholic schools and graduated from U. Mass (Boston) in 1971. She moved to New York in 1974 to be a poet. She gave her first reading at CBGB's and then gravitated to St. Mark's Church where she studied with Paul Violi, Alice Notley and Ted Berrigan. She edited a poetry magazine *dodgems* in 1977–79. She ran the Saint Mark's Poetry Project in 1984–86. She's written two plays, *Feeling Blue, Parts 1, 2 & 3* and *Modern Art*, both of which were performed at P.S. 122. With Liz Kotz she edited *The New Fuck You / adventures in lesbian reading* (Semiotext(e) 1995) which won a Lambda Book Award. Black Sparrow Press has published Eileen Myles's book of short stories *Chelsea Girls* (1994) and a book of poems, *Maxfield Parrish* (1995). Her most recent book of poems from Black Sparrow is *School of Fish* (1997).